MW00593743

QUOTES FOR WOMEN

BY WOMEN

Applewood Books
Carlisle, Massachusetts

"We ask justice, we ask equality, we ask that all the civil and political rights that belong to citizens of the United States, be guaranteed to us and our daughters forever."

– Declaration of Rights for Women, July 1876

"Votes for Women," an inspiration for this book of quotations, was a popular slogan in the campaign for women's suffrage in the United States. Winning the right to vote is just one of the many challenges women have faced throughout the generations in their quest for equality.

Women—our mothers, sisters, daughters, aunts, nieces, mentors, and friends, make up more than 50 percent of the American population and have always played an integral role in the history of our country and the world. Whether it be contributions in science, business, medicine, the military, and education; marching for equal rights and participating in the suffragette movement; raising our future leaders; fighting in our wars or fighting for equal pay and breaking through the ever-present glass ceiling—throughout time women have made an enormous impact on our world. Today, there are few areas in society where women do not play a critical role. Girls growing up now have career and life choices that were not an option in the past and in many instances are far beyond the dreams of our mothers and grandmothers.

Through these quotes—spoken by the great women of our time as well as those from our past—we hear the passion and commitment they express as their words guide future generations and support them along the path of their lives. These women teach us that it starts on the inside—in the unique, individual woman herself. In order to create change, women must perceive themselves as truly worthy—and value the gift they can contribute to the world.

"How important it is to recognize and celebrate our heroes and she-roes."

– Maya Angelou

"I long to hear that you have declared an independency—and by the way in the new Code of Laws which I suppose it will be necessary for you to make I desire you would Remember the Ladies, and be more generous and favourable to them than your ancestors. Do not put such unlimited power into the hands of the Husbands. Remember all Men would be tyrants if they could."
– Abigail Adams, First Lady, in a letter to John Adams, 1776

— *Sf Sf Sf* —

"I do not wish [women] to have power over men, but over themselves."
– Mary Wollstonecraft, mother of Mary Shelley and author of *Vindication of the Rights of Women*, 1792

— *Sf Sf Sf* —

"Habit and Hope are the crutches which support us through the vicissitudes of life."
– Dolley Madison, First Lady, 1848

"Woman stock is rising in the market. I shall not live to see women vote, but I'll come and rap on the ballot box."

– Lydia Maria Child, American women's rights activist, from *Letter to Sarah Shaw*, 1856

"Lovely weather so far; I don't know how long it will last, but I'm not afraid of storms, for I'm learning how to sail my ship."

– Louisa May Alcott, writer, *Little Women*, 1869

"It seems that life is not easy for any of us. But what of that? We must have perseverance and above all confidence in ourselves. We must believe that we are gifted for something, and that this thing, at whatever cost, must be attained."

– Marie Curie, winner of the 1903 Nobel Prize in Physics and the 1911 Nobel Prize in Chemistry, letter to her brother, March 18, 1894

"It is not easy to be a pioneer—but oh, it is fascinating! I would not trade one moment, even the worst moment, for all the riches in the world."

– Elizabeth Blackwell, first female M.D. in the U.S., from her autobiography *Pioneer Work in Opening the Medical Profession to Women*, 1895

— ꒡ ꒡ ꒡ —

"In a word, I am always busy, which is perhaps the chief reason why I am always well."

– Elizabeth Cady Stanton, women's rights activist, diary, December 3, 1901

— ꒡ ꒡ ꒡ —

"Optimism is the faith that leads to achievement; nothing can be done without hope."

– Helen Keller, humanitarian, *Optimism*, 1903

— ꒡ ꒡ ꒡ —

"I think the girl who is able to earn her own living and pay her own way should be as happy as anybody on earth. The sense of independence and security is very sweet."

– Susan B. Anthony, women's rights activist, *New York Press* interview, February 26, 1905

"I hope I'll never get ambitious enough to try anything. It's so much nicer to be damned sure I could do it better than other people—and I might not if I tried. That of course would break my heart— "

– Zelda Fitzgerald, socialite and writer, from a letter to her husband, F. Scott Fitzgerald, 1919

—❦❦❦—

"Beware of monotony; it's the mother of all the deadly sins."

– Edith Wharton, writer, *The Age of Innocence*, 1920

—❦❦❦—

"I would venture to guess that Anon, who wrote so many poems without signing them, was often a woman."

– Virginia Wolff, writer, *A Room of One's Own*, 1929

—❦❦❦—

"I want to do it because I want to do it. Women must try to do things as men have tried. When they fail, their failure must be but a challenge to others."

– Amelia Earhart, American aviation pioneer and author in a letter to her husband, written in case a dangerous flight proved to be her last, 1937

"A woman has got to love a bad man once or twice in her life, to be thankful for a good one."
– Marjorie Kinnan Rawlings, writer, *The Yearling,* 1939

— *𝒮𝒮𝒮* —

"Life shrinks or expands in proportion with one's courage."
– Anaïs Nin, writer, Diary, June 1941

— *𝒮𝒮𝒮* —

"Men put me down as the best woman painter ... I think I'm one of the best painters."
– Georgia O'Keeffe, artist, *Women of Achievement: Georgia O'Keeffe,* 1943

— *𝒮𝒮𝒮* —

"You grow up the day you have your first real laugh—at yourself."
– Ethel Barrymore, actress, *Cosmopolitan* interview, 1943

— *𝒮𝒮𝒮* —

"As long as you keep a person down, some part of you has to be down there to hold him down, so it means you cannot soar as you might otherwise."
– Marian Anderson, singer, paraphrasing Booker T. Washington, CBS TV, December 30, 1957

"Courage is more exhilarating than fear and in the long run it is easier."
– Eleanor Roosevelt, First Lady, *You Learn by Living*, 1960

—✧✧✧—

"No matter what accomplishments you make, somebody helps you."
– Wilma Rudolph, winner of three gold medals in the 1960 Summer Olympics, 1960

—✧✧✧—

"Nothing is impossible, the word itself says, 'I'm possible'!"
– Audrey Hepburn, actress, humanitarian, 1962

—✧✧✧—

"In politics, if you want anything said, ask a man; if you want anything done, ask a woman."
– Margaret Thatcher, first female prime minister of the United Kingdom, speech to the National Union of Townswomen, Royal Albert Hall, May 20, 1965

"The environment after all is where we all meet; where all have a mutual interest; it is the one thing all of us share. It is not only a mirror of ourselves, but a focusing lens on what we can become."

– Lady Bird Johnson, First Lady, speech at Yale University, White House Diary, October 9, 1967

— ⚘ ⚘ ⚘ —

"In order to be irreplaceable one must always be different."

– Coco Chanel, fashion designer, interview with Michael Haedrich, *Coco Chanel: Her Life, Her Secrets*, 1971

— ⚘ ⚘ ⚘ —

"Change your life today. Don't gamble on the future, act now, without delay."

– Simone de Beauvoir, writer and philosopher, interview with Alice Schwarzer, "I Am a Feminist," 1972

— ⚘ ⚘ ⚘ —

"Of my two 'handicaps,' being female put many more obstacles in my path than being black."

– Shirley Chisholm, politician and educator, reported in "Shirley Chisholm Kicks Off Campaign for U.S. Presidency" by Ronald E. Kisner, *Jet*, vol. 41, no. 20, February 1972

"I think self-awareness is probably the most important thing toward being a champion."

– Billie Jean King, tennis star, in *Sportswoman,* November/
December 1973

"Of course, we all must realize that the path to peace may be a little bit difficult, but not as difficult as the path to war."

– Golda Meir, prime minister of Israel, during the 1977 visit from
Anwar Sadat, president of Egypt

"You take your life in your own hands, and what happens? A terrible thing: no one to blame."

– Erica Jong, writer, *How to Save Your Own Life,* 1977

"And when we speak we are afraid our words will not be heard nor welcomed. But when we are silent, we are still afraid. So it is better to speak."

– Audre Lorde, writer, "A Litany for Survival," *The Black Unicorn,* 1978

"A strong woman is a woman determined to do something others are determined not be done."

– Marge Piercy, writer, "For Strong Women," *The Moon Is Always Female,* 1980

— ❦ ❦ ❦ —

"Where there's love and inspiration, I don't think you could ever go wrong."

– Ella Fitzgerald, singer, in the *Boston Globe*, February 17, 1982

— ❦ ❦ ❦ —

"Dying seems less sad than having lived too little."

– Gloria Steinem, journalist, "Ruth's Story (Because She Could Not Say It)," *Outrageous Acts & Everyday Rebellions*, 1983

— ❦ ❦ ❦ —

"If you're offered a seat on a rocket ship, don't ask what seat. Just get on."

– Christa McAuliffe, astronaut and teacher on Space Shuttle Challenger, while on the *Tonight Show Starring Johnny Carson*, 1985

"I did not get there by wishing for it, or dreaming about it, or hoping for it. I got there by working for it."

– Estée Lauder, businesswoman, in the *Boston Globe*, December 8, 1985

—⁂—

"If you obey all the rules you miss all the fun."

– Katharine Hepburn, actress, *The Making of* The African Queen; *or How I Went to Africa with Bogart, Bacall and Huston and Almost Lost My Mind*, 1987

—⁂—

"And if you can't go straight ahead, you go around the corner."

– Cher, singer and actress, in *Cosmopolitan*, February 1988

—⁂—

"A woman is the full circle. Within her is the ability to create, nurture, and transform."

– Diane Mariechild, women's spirituality writer, *Mother Wit*, July 1988

"My father knew you can imprison a man, but not an idea. You can exile a man, but not an idea. You can kill a man, but not an idea."

– Benazir Bhutto, prime minister of Pakistan, *Daughter of Destiny*, 1989

— *˄ ˄ ˄* —

"Every dance is a kind of fever chart, a graph of the heart. Desire is a lovely thing, and that is where the dance comes from, from desire."

– Martha Graham, dancer, from her autobiography, *Blood Memory*, 1991

— *˄ ˄ ˄* —

"I'm tough, I'm ambitious, and I know exactly what I want. If that makes me a bitch, OK."

– Madonna, singer and actress, in *People*, July 27, 1992

— *˄ ˄ ˄* —

"I believe I'm here for a reason. And I think a little bit of the reason is to throw little torches out to the next step to lead people through the dark."

– Whoopi Goldberg, actress, in *Parade*, November 1, 1992

"Don't be limited by others' limited imaginations."

– Mae C. Jemison, first female African American astronaut, in the *New York Times*, March 3, 1993

—❦❦❦—

"Don't look at your feet to see if you are doing it right. Just dance."

– Anne Lamott, writer, *Bird by Bird*, 1994

—❦❦❦—

"I have learned over the years that when one's mind is made up, this diminishes fear; knowing what must be done does away with fear."

– Rosa Parks, civil rights activist, *Quiet Strength*, 1994

—❦❦❦—

"Aging is not 'lost youth,' but a new stage of opportunity and strength."

– Betty Friedan, women's rights activist, "How to Live Longer, Better, Wiser," *Parade,* March 20, 1994

—❦❦❦—

"If you find someone you love in life, you must hang on to that love and look after it."

– Diana, Princess of Wales, BBC *Panorama* interview, November 20, 1995

"Above all, be the heroine of your life, not the victim."

– Nora Ephron, writer, "Commencement Address to Wellesley Class of 1996," May 1996

"If your actions create a legacy that inspires others to dream more, learn more, do more and become more, then, you are an excellent leader."

– Dolly Parton, singer and actress, in *The Most Important Thing I Know,* 1997

"Every single one of us matters, has a role to play, makes a difference. We cannot live through a day without impacting the world around us— and we have a choice: what sort of impact do we want to make?"

– Jane Goodall, primatologist, *Reason for Hope: A Spiritual Journey,* 1999

"If you think that caring for yourself is selfish, change your mind, because you are simply ducking your responsibilities."

– Ann Richards, governor of Texas, speaking to the Michigan Menopause Action Team, September 23, 1999

"Drama is very important in life: You have to come on with a bang. You never want to go out with a whimper. Everything can have drama if it's done right—even a pancake."

– Julia Child, chef, *Esquire* interview, June 2000

— ✑✑✑ —

"Women will only have true equality when men share with them the responsibility of bringing up the next generation."

– Ruth Bader Ginsburg, Supreme Court justice, conversation with Lynn Sherr of ABC before the members of the New York Bar Association, November 15, 2000

— ✑✑✑ —

"Take criticism seriously, but not personally. If there is truth or merit in the criticism, try to learn from it. Otherwise, let it roll right off you."

– Hillary Rodham Clinton, First Lady, senator, and secretary of state, *Living History*, 2003

— ✑✑✑ —

"I know for sure that what we dwell on is who we become—as a woman thinks, so she is."

– Oprah Winfrey, talk show host, actress, and media entrepreneur, in *O, The Oprah Magazine*, July 2003

"Figure out who you are separate from your family and the man or woman you're in a relationship with. Find who you are in this world and what you need to feel good alone. I think that's the most important thing in life. Find a sense of self because with that, you can do anything else."

– Angelina Jolie, actress, philanthropist, and humanitarian, *Cosmopolitan* interview, August 2003

— *√ √ √* —

"See your mothering as a political act. The way you talk to your child becomes his or her inner voice."

– Peggy O'Mara, editor of *Mothering* magazine, *Mothering*, January-February 2005

— *√ √ √* —

"A good compromise is one where everybody makes a contribution."

– Angela Merkel, chancellor of Germany, *Financial Times* interview, June 2005

— *√ √ √* —

"You can't please everyone, and you can't make everyone like you."

– Katie Couric, news anchor, in *Ladies Home Journal*, October 2005

"See, now that's your problem, you're wishin' too much baby. You gotta stop wearing your wishbone where your backbone oughta be."
– Elizabeth Gilbert, writer, *Eat Pray Love*, 2006

— ༄ ༄ ༄ —

"We do not need magic to change the world, we carry all the power we need inside ourselves already: we have the power to imagine better."
– J. K. Rowling, writer, "The Fringe Benefits of Failure, and the Importance of Imagination," Harvard University Commencement Address, June 5, 2008

— ༄ ༄ ༄ —

"When I'm tired, I rest. I say, 'I can't be a superwoman today.' "
– Jada Pinkett Smith, actress, *Redbook* interview, January 2009

— ༄ ༄ ༄ —

"Everything bad that's ever happened to me has taught me compassion."
– Ellen DeGeneres, comedian and talk show host, on the *Oprah Winfrey Show*, November 9, 2009

"What you are doing I cannot do, what I'm doing you cannot do, but together we are doing something beautiful."

– Mother Teresa, Catholic nun and missionary named Saint Teresa of Calcutta, from *Where There Is Love, There Is God*, published 2010

— ⸎ ⸎ ⸎ —

"I strongly believe you never should spend your time being the former anything."

– Condoleezza Rice, secretary of state, *Harvard Business Review* interview, January-February 2010

— ⸎ ⸎ ⸎ —

"Some women choose to follow men, and some women choose to follow their dreams. If you're wondering which way to go, remember that your career will never wake up and tell you that it doesn't love you anymore."

– Lady Gaga, singer, in *Cosmopolitan*, April 2010

— ⸎ ⸎ ⸎ —

"All careers go up and down like friendships, like marriages, like anything else, and you can't bat a thousand all the time."

– Julie Andrews, singer and actress, *The Telegraph* interview, May 4, 2010

"It took me quite a long time to develop a voice, and now that I have it, I am not going to be silent."

– Madeleine Albright, first female secretary of state, *Huffington Post* interview, June 2010

— *§§§* —

"I feel if in your *mind* you can do it, you can do it. You cannot doubt yourself. Doubt is a killer. You just have to know who you are and what you stand for."

– Jennifer Lopez, actress and singer, *Glamour* interview, August 2010

— *§§§* —

"The challenge is not to be perfect. It's to be whole."

– Jane Fonda, actress, on the *Oprah Winfrey Show*, October 27, 2010

— *§§§* —

"I hope the fathers and mothers of little girls will look at them and say 'yes, women can.' "

– Dilma Rousseff, first female president of Brazil, victory speech, October 31, 2010

"You can't be that kid standing at the top of the waterslide, overthinking it. You have to go down the chute."

– Tina Fey, comedian and writer, *Bossy Pants*, 2011

— ⚜ ⚜ ⚜ —

"Whenever you are blue or lonely or stricken by some humiliating thing you did, the cure and the hope is in caring about other people."

– Diane Sawyer, news anchor, on *Oprah's Master Class*,
January 2, 2011

— ⚜ ⚜ ⚜ —

"I just love bossy women. I could be around them all day. To me, bossy is not a pejorative term at all. It means somebody's passionate and engaged and ambitious and doesn't mind learning."

– Amy Poehler, comedian, *Glamour* interview, April 2011

"Do not bring people in your life who weigh you down. And trust your instincts. You know, good relationships feel good. They feel right. They don't hurt. They're not painful. That's not just with somebody you want to marry, but it's with the friends that you choose. It's with the people you surround yourselves with."

– Michelle Obama, First Lady, remarks at an event with Elizabeth Garrett Anderson students, Oxford University, May 25, 2011

"There's nothing wrong with being afraid. It's not the absence of fear, it's overcoming it. Sometimes you've got to blast through and have faith."

– Emma Watson, actress, press conference, New York City, July 10, 2011

"This journey has always been about reaching your own other shore no matter what it is, and that dream continues."

– Diana Nyad, long-distance swimmer, upon ending her third attempt to swim from Cuba to Florida, September 25, 2011

"Everyone shines, given the right lighting."

– Susan Cain, author of *Quiet: The Power of Introverts in a World that Can't Stop Talking*, *Forbes* interview, January 27, 2012

— *// // //* —

"If you're someone people count on, particularly in difficult moments, that's a sign of a life lived honorably."

– Rachel Maddow, news anchor, *O, The Oprah Magazine* interview, March 2012

— *// // //* —

"If you're not making mistakes, then you're not making decisions."

– Catherine Cook, founded myYearbook at age fifteen, *Inc.* interview, April 2012

— *// // //* —

"And I was smart enough to go through any door that opened."

– Joan Rivers, comedian, *Fresh Air* interview, June 11, 2012

"Most people don't place their relationship as high in priorities as things like business. You should treat your marriage like a business that you wouldn't want to let fail."

– Lisa Ling, journalist, Redbook interview, October 2012

"When I believe in something, I'm like a dog with a bone."

– Melissa McCarthy, comedian, *Good Housekeeping* interview, November 2012

"Women have to work much harder to make it in this world. It really pisses me off that women don't get the same opportunities as men do, or money for that matter. Because let's face it, money gives men the power to run the show. It gives men the power to define our values and to define what's sexy and what's feminine and that's bullshit. At the end of the day, it's not about equal rights, it's about how we think. We have to reshape our own perception of how we view ourselves."

– Beyoncé Knowles Carter, singer, *Life Is But a Dream*, HBO documentary, 2013

"When looking for a life partner, my advice to women is date all of them: the bad boys, the cool boys, the commitment-phobic boys, the crazy boys. But do not marry them. The things that make the bad boys sexy do not make them good husbands. When it comes time to settle down, find someone who wants an equal partner. Someone who thinks women should be smart, opinionated and ambitious. Someone who values fairness and expects or, even better, wants to do his share in the home. These men exist and, trust me, over time, nothing is sexier."

– Sheryl Sandberg, COO of Facebook, *Lean In*, 2013

— ♮ ♮ ♮ —

"The girls who were unanimously considered beautiful often rested on their beauty alone. I felt I had to do things, to be intelligent and develop a personality in order to be seen as attractive. By the time I realized maybe I wasn't plain and might even possibly be pretty, I had already trained myself to be a little more interesting and informed."

– Diane von Furstenberg, fashion designer, *Diane: A Signature Life*, 2013

"I learned that I need to listen well so that I hear what is not said."

– Thuli Madonsela, human rights lawyer, *Corruption Watch* interview, March 8, 2013

—⚜⚜⚜—

"A surplus of effort could overcome a deficit of confidence."

– Sonia Sotomayor, Supreme Court justice, *My Beloved World*, 2013

—⚜⚜⚜—

"It's one of the greatest gifts you can give to yourself…forgive. Forgive everybody."

– Maya Angelou, poet, Oprah Winfrey's *Super Soul Sunday* interview, May 12, 2013

—⚜⚜⚜—

"Refuse to be in the shadows as you step out into this life. Don't be shy no matter how crazy it seems to you. That crazy idea may just be the solution for some crazy global or local problem."

– Leymah Gbowee, activist and 2011 Nobel Peace Prize winner, Barnard College commencement, New York City, May 19, 2013

"You have [to] trust in what you think. If you splinter yourself and try to please everyone, you can't."

– Annie Leibovitz, photographer, *Fast Company* interview, June 2013

— *¼ ¼ ¼* —

"When the whole world is silent, even one voice becomes powerful."

– Malala Yousafzai, education activist, Harvard Foundation Peter J. Gomes Award acceptance speech, September 27, 2013

— *¼ ¼ ¼* —

"Women asking for raises should not only know their value, but they should ask with the confidence that they're helping the company to be successful."

– Kirsten Gillibrand, senator, *Glamour* interview, March 11, 2014

"I'm always perpetually out of my comfort zone."
– Tory Burch, fashion designer, WTOP interview, July 23, 2014

—⚜⚜⚜—

"If you're a feminist...you believe that men and women should have the same opportunities. If you are a feminist, you're for equal rights on the whole. That's not a concept you can really shoot down."
– Lena Dunham, actress and writer, Just for Laughs 42 Toronto Comedy Festival interview, September 20, 2014

—⚜⚜⚜—

"If somebody can do something 80 percent as good as you think you would have done it yourself, then you've got to let it go."
– Sara Blakely, founder of Spanx, *Marie Claire* interview, November 4, 2014

"We teach girls to shrink themselves, to make themselves smaller. We say to girls: 'You can have ambition, but not too much. You should aim to be successful, but not too successful. Otherwise, you will threaten the man.' Because I am female, I am expected to aspire to marriage. I am expected to make my life choices, always keeping in mind that marriage is the most important. Now, marriage can be a source of joy and love and mutual support, but why do we teach girls to aspire to marriage and we don't teach boys the same?"

– Chimamanda Ngozi Adichie, writer, *We Should All Be Feminists*, 2015

— ✓ ✓ ✓ —

"I try to live in a little bit of my own joy and not let people steal it or take it."

– Hoda Kotb, news anchor, *Huffington Post* interview, January 12, 2015

"A feminist is a person who believes in the power of women just as much as they believe in the power of anyone else. It's equality, it's fairness, and I think it's a great thing to be a part of."

– Zendaya, actress and singer, *Flare* magazine interview, November 2015

— ✦✦✦ —

"I really think a champion is defined not by their wins, but by how they can recover when they fall."

– Serena Williams, after winning her 22nd grand slam title in tennis, July 2016

— ✦✦✦ —

"You can be the lead in your own life."

– Kerry Washington, actress, *Glamour* interview, October 2016